SUPER SKILLS

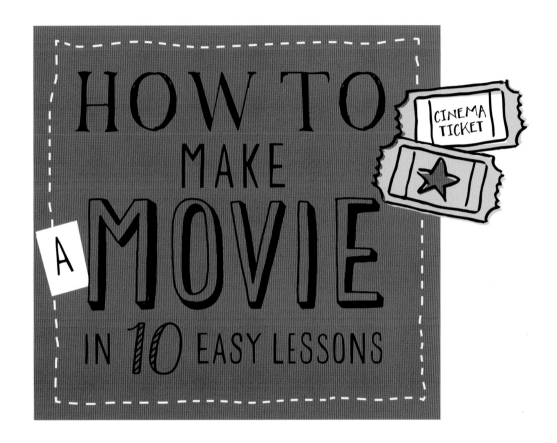

HOW TO MAKE A MOVIE
IN 10 EASY LESSONS

ROBERT BLOFIELD

QED Publishing

ABOUT THE AUTHOR

Robert Blofield is an independent filmmaker and film production teacher from Hampshire, UK. He began creating independent video productions for film festivals and freelance projects in 2005 and, since becoming enthralled with the medium, has gone on to teach professional film and television production techniques to a new generation of filmmakers. Robert is currently in the pre-production stages of three fictional shorts, which he will be directing and unveiling at major film festivals in 2015/16.

Publisher: Zeta Jones
Art Director: Susi Martin
Managing Editor: Laura Knowles
Design: Punch Bowl Design
Original illustrations: Venetia Dean

Picture credits (t=top, b=bottom, l=left, r=right, c=centre)
Shutterstock 2b 62b LHF Graphics, 3 15 16 1718 20 21t 23 24 36b 41b 49b 61b 62b Monkik, 3tr 3tl 6t 12t 20t 26t 30t 40t 46t 50t 56t 60t Lyudmyla Kharlamova, 4l Igorij, 5l 59c zayats-and-zayats, 6c 7r 12 21b 27t 28 43 61t Paisit Teeraphatsakool,9r Jesus Sanz, 14 15 Oxy_gen & benchart & Budi Susanto, 20b Punch Bowl Design, 27b Ohn Mar, 30b Actor, 32 33 34b 35 Artisticco, 54 xenia_ok, 57t 57b JanPetrskovsky, 59t Yurlick, 62c zeber.

CONTENTS

WELCOME TO THE WORLD OF MOVIES

So you want to be a filmmaker? It's not as difficult as you might think! Like most things, it just takes some dedication and practice to unlock your potential. In this book we will look at the key skills that all budding filmmakers use to turn their ideas into reality and make great movies. As you read, that idea you've got in your head will begin to grow into a well-rounded project, ready for you to go and shoot. And that's exactly what we'll then go and do.

Are you ready?

I'll be covering everything you need to know in order to make your first film, and at this stage it doesn't really matter what type of film you want to make. The most important thing is that you're up for experimenting with making a film. Some things might work, others might not. This book will help you figure out the best way to end up with a fantastic film.

'WOW' FACTOR!

IT DOESN'T MATTER IF YOUR FILM IS A FICTIONAL DRAMA, DOCUMENTARY, ANIMATION PROJECT, OR ANYTHING IN BETWEEN. MANY OF THE SKILLS AND TECHNIQUES IN THIS BOOK APPLY TO ALL GENRES.

HOW DOES IT WORK?

I've put together a set of ten core skills that we'll look at one by one. The order of these skills follows the natural flow of making a film, so that when we're working on the project we are moving in the right direction. I'll teach you everything you need to know, and in the right order to get your project moving.

This book has been written as not only a guide to the techniques, but also as a shopping list of what it takes to successfully make your first movie. If you learn the skills and have your project follow the order we'll go through, you should end up making the film you want.

ANYONE CAN DO IT

Not too many years ago, the technology needed to shoot professional-looking films was extremely expensive. But now we live in a completely different world. When I head off down to the shops I carry with me a high quality, portable video recorder capable of shooting all manner of lighting situations in full HD: my smartphone. What is so fantastic about this piece of technology is that despite its small size, if it's used correctly it is capable of recording images that are 'TV ready'. So for the first time ever, it really doesn't matter what equipment you have available to you - anyone can make a movie.

LOCAL FILM FESTIVAL
WORLD PREMIER
YOUR SHORT FILM
TONIGHT ONLY

HANDY TIP!
Make a habit of taking video or photos of anything that interests you. Write down any ideas that come to you in a notebook or phone app. Practising these skills will make you the best filmmaker you can be.

THE MOST IMPORTANT THING TO DO WHEN MAKING A FILM IS TO ENJOY YOURSELF! NOW,
LET'S BEGIN...

FIND INSPIRATION

We all love stories. Now it's your turn to tell one! At the beginning of all film projects you're faced with two big questions. The first is, what medium do you want to use? Your film can be fiction, documentary, stop-motion animation, a music video or one of dozens of other choices. The second question is, what story do you want to tell?

GETTING STARTED

The writing stage is one of the most fundamental parts of your film. You should try to make this part good, but don't spend too much time on it, as we want to keep up the pace and move through all the stages of filmmaking. I'm a firm believer in getting what we need completed and then moving on before getting bogged down.

Once you've answered these questions, have a look at what you've written. I think it's a great idea to use this as the starting point for your first film. Some people might try to make a certain type of film because it's popular, or they think that their friends will like it. But you'll probably make the best film if it's a type that you truly love.

HANDY TIP!
Ask yourself the questions on this list and write down your answers.

What types of films do I like?
ACTION ADVENTURE ROMANCE
HORROR DRAMA HISTORICAL
COMEDY SCI-FI OTHER

What is my favourite film?

Why do I like this film?
THE ACTORS THE SCRIPT
THE SITUATIONS THE VISUALS OTHER

How does this film make me feel?
SCARED HAPPY
EXCITED SAD OTHER

ACTION

WHAT DOES A STORY NEED?

Whether we're making something fictional like a drama or a stop-motion animation, or something factual like a documentary, there's always a story to tell. And it's your job to tell it! Think about your story and begin to put a few ideas down on paper.

SHAPING THE STORY

By now, we should have some basic ideas that will help to shape the story. We know what type of film we're going to make, how it should make us feel, what aspects of other films we would like to include and now we know something about the characters in the story.

This is enough basic information to get a simplified picture of the film as a whole. We'll use this information to make the simplest possible write-up of your story so that you can begin working on the script.

Who are the main characters in my story?

What is their goal?

Why are they interesting?

Where do they end up?

How do they get there?

WRITE A TWEET (JUST 140 CHARACTERS) THAT DESCRIBES EVERYTHING YOU NEED TO KNOW ABOUT YOUR FILM AND THE BASIC PLOT. IT'S CHALLENGING, BUT IT WILL REALLY HELP YOU PINPOINT THE MOST IMPORTANT FEATURES OF YOUR FILM IDEA.

WHAT'S IT GOING TO LOOK LIKE?

Ok, so now we know what your film is all about. Great! We're almost ready to begin planning the film properly. There is one more area that we should look at before we move on. It might make you rethink your ideas, so it's better to address this now rather than later on.

PRODUCTION VALUE

'Production value' is a term we use to describe how professional a project looks. If a project looks like it has been professionally made, then the audience recognises the film as being of high production value. But if the audience picks up on elements they see as amateur, they switch off.

Your job is to maximise the production value of the film. This means making it look as professional as possible. Here are a few tips that can help with this. These are just guidelines, and they don't have to be followed to the letter. But thinking about these issues before you start shooting can help make your film look great.

Tip 1: CHOOSE THE RIGHT SETTING

You might have everything you need to turn a small room into the bridge of a spaceship. If you do, then your film could look fantastic! On the other hand, if your sets are made of cardboard and sticky tape, your film might look a bit rubbish. I would advise that your story take place in a location you can easily recreate.

'WOW' FACTOR!

MAYBE YOU CAN'T MAKE A FILM SET IN A PALACE, BUT YOU CAN MAKE A TRULY SCARY FILM SET IN A CREEPY ABANDONED BUILDING BY MOVING ITEMS AROUND IN YOUR LOFT.

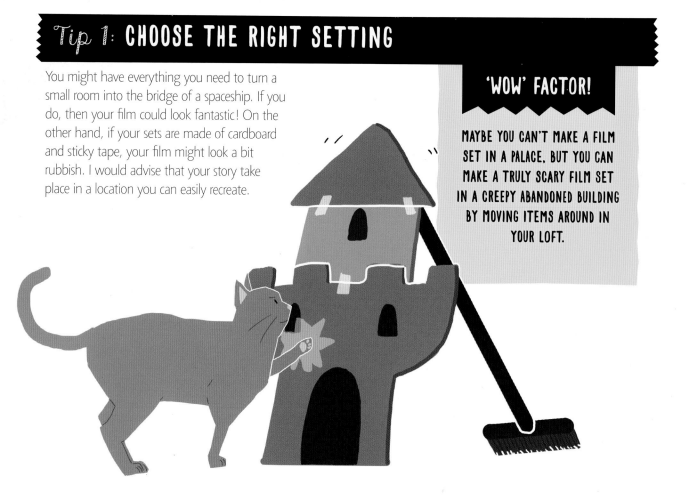

Tip 2: MAKE YOUR PROPS STAND OUT

A plain tea or coffee mug is not particularly exciting; everyone has them in their kitchen. If you have access to an object that is more unusual, try to use it as a prop. I've seen items such as gas masks, antique work uniforms and old computers used in my students' films, giving them a much higher production value. These items are not everyday, but they aren't impossible to get hold of, either.

HANDY TIP!
You can search car boot sales and charity shops for unusual items to use in your film.

Tip 3: SMALLER IS BETTER

IT'S ALWAYS BEST TO TRY AND MAKE A SHORT FILM OF NO MORE THAN 10 MINUTES AS YOUR FIRST PROJECT. BY KEEPING IT SHORT YOU'LL COMPLETE IT MUCH FASTER. THEN YOU CAN START YOUR NEXT PROJECT!

The more characters you have, the more work it will be to plan the project. Chances are that if you've got too many characters to plan for, more things will go wrong on the shoot, which can affect the overall film.

Tip 4: ACT YOUR AGE

If your only actors are young people, it might look odd if they are playing 40-year-olds in your film. So a courtroom drama might not be the best choice! However, a film about a group of kids finding a buried treasure map or going on an adventure would work just fine.

HANDY TIP!
Leave your audience wanting more! Your story should have an ending, but try leaving it open for a possible sequel.

BE CREATIVE

Now that you've had a think about what your film will look like, you might want to refine your idea a little bit. You don't necessarily need to change it completely; remember that stories can be told in many different ways. With a bit of creative thinking, you can tell your story in a way that doesn't require a huge special-effects budget!

'WOW' FACTOR!

THERE HAVE BEEN SOME REALLY BRILLIANT SCI-FI AND HORROR FILMS MADE IN WHICH THE MONSTER IS HARDLY SHOWN AT ALL. THE DRAMA AND SUSPENSE COME FROM THE HUMAN CHARACTERS' RESPONSES TO IT.

LEARNING LESSONS

Making your film is going to be a learning exercise. You will learn almost everything you need to know from making your first film, and it is probably the single most valuable bit of training in making movies you'll ever get. It is something that everyone can do, but it will take dedication and some hard work to make the film great.

You will learn a lot of lessons while working on your project, both positive and negative. The positive things are ones you will do again, because they worked well. As for the negative things… well, that's really just a polite term for failures. Some are major and some are minor, but you can learn from all of them. It's all part of the process!

HANDY TIP!

If you're happy and excited about telling the story you have planned, then go with it. It's incredibly important that you believe in the project and that you are excited to make it.

WHAT'S MY MOTIVATION?

Think about what you want to get out of making a film. Is it to impress your friends? Become rich and famous? Or do you have a story in your head that just needs to be told? If you know why you want to make a particular film, your passion will shine through.

DON'T EXPECT THINGS TO GO PERFECTLY ON YOUR FIRST SHOOT. WHEN THEY GO WRONG, DON'T LET IT STOP YOU. JUST BE PREPARED TO THINK OF A SOLUTION.

Lastly, I want you to set some personal goals for the film. Think about a film, TV series, director or writer that has inspired you to try filmmaking. Then identify three small points from your inspiration that you want to work towards on this project. It could be to have a really high-tension, dramatic conversation on screen, or to have a really fast-paced chase scene, or even to shoot a scene from an unusual angle. Whatever you might want to achieve, make a note of it now. We'll come back to it later.

TURN YOUR IDEA INTO A SCRIPT

We're going to take this as a fairly relaxed approach to writing your first script. You don't need to worry about formatting it exactly the same way that Hollywood writers do, but the example I show here is fairly close. By using this template you'll be getting into good habits for your future projects. If your script is written in a way that's easy to understand, chances are your film will also be easy to follow.

THE SECTIONS OF YOUR SCRIPT

Each scene will consist of three elements: scene headings, action and dialogue. This sample script shows you how they are used. The scene is one where a young boy is attracted to a shimmering object hidden at the back of a dark cellar.

This scene heading tells us the location that the scene takes place in and the time of day.

The action describes what will be happening on screen. It also hints that the scene is mysterious and doesn't give us any information about what the boy has found.

Each character's lines are centre-aligned to make them easier to spot, and they begin with the character's name.

IF YOU USE A STANDARD LAYOUT WHEN YOU FORMAT YOUR SCRIPT, IT WILL HELP TO ORGANISE YOUR THOUGHTS AND MAKE IT EASIER FOR YOUR ACTORS TO UNDERSTAND THE STORY.

DARK CELLAR — AFTERNOON

A young boy is exploring a dark, cold cellar. A weak glowing light crosses his face, coming from an object hidden behind an old cabinet at the back of the room. He moves towards it to investigate.

YOUNG BOY
What the...

As the boy approaches the cabinet we see the shimmering light on his face grow stronger and a look of astonishment creep across his face.

YOUNG BOY
No way!

We hear footsteps coming from the cellar stairs. The boy quickly hides the mysterious item in the cabinet before spinning around to see his mother standing midway down the staircase.

MOTHER
There you are! Dinner's ready.

GOLDEN RULES

When you're writing a script, always make it clear:

• where and when the scene is taking place

• what is happening on screen

• who is talking and what they are saying.

NOW IT'S YOUR TURN!

Think about your story idea and break it down into scenes. What filmmakers call a scene is a part of the story that takes place in one location in 'real time'. This means that if you change location, or skip forwards or backwards in time, you need a new scene.

Once you've broken your film into its scenes, start writing. You might make changes as you go along, but usually once you have begun writing, this stage picks up speed and you'll find the story is completed in no time.

AS A VERY ROUGH RULE OF THUMB, ONE PAGE OF SCREENPLAY LASTS ABOUT A MINUTE ONCE IT'S SHOT. BUT THIS DEPENDS ON HOW MUCH DESCRIPTION YOUR SCRIPT INCLUDES, OR HOW QUICK-FIRE THE DIALOGUE IS.

A torch or another battery-powered light source can be hidden within your scene to illuminate important objects within the story.

By using this over-the-shoulder shot, we can see a great deal of the scene's layout from one character's perspective.

HANDY TIP!

The audience doesn't need to see characters greeting each other or saying goodbye. You can just cut into each scene once the important stuff is happening and leave as it ends.

TYPES OF SHOTS

The most important stage of your idea's development is coming up now: you need to start planning to shoot your film. When talking about different shots, there are some terms that we usually use to help get our ideas across. This is where shot sizes and angles come in: they help to describe the shot in a way that all filmmakers understand. Here some of the standard shot sizes used in films.

MAKE SURE YOUR FRIENDS KNOW THESE TERMS. IT WILL MAKE WORKING TOGETHER MUCH EASIER!

CLOSE-UP

Everyone has heard of a close-up. It's a shot that is zoomed in to feature only the face of the character. It's a good way of showing emotion.

LONG SHOT/WIDE ANGLE

This is a zoomed-out shot that frames a character from at least head to toe. It can also be used to frame someone from very far away so that they are very small on screen. Anything between these two extremes is known as a long shot or wide angle shot.

MEDIUM SHOT

Also called a 'mid-shot', this frames a character from the waist up to just past their head. It shows the audience the character's expression and body language, and is very often used in dialogue scenes.

MORE SHOT SIZES AND ANGLES

Close-up, mid-shot and wide angle are the shots that are most commonly used. But there are other types of shots that can be used to create interesting effects. Try not to over-use them, otherwise they will have have less of an effect.

HANDY TIP!
An extreme close-up is a great way to show fear or other intense emotion.

EXTREME CLOSE-UP:

This is a more zoomed-in version of the close-up. Rather than being able to see only the character's face, we will only see part of the face, such as the eyes.

MEDIUM CLOSE-UP:

This one is halfway between a mid-shot and a close-up. It usually shows just the character's head and shoulders or chest.

MEDIUM LONG SHOT:

A shot that frames almost the full character, from the knees up.

HIGH ANGLE SHOT:

You can place the camera above the height of the character, looking down on them. This can often make the character seem vulnerable or weaker in the frame, or show the point of view of another character looking down from above.

LOW ANGLE SHOT:

The opposite of a high angle shot, this is shot from a position lower than the character looking up. This can make the character seem taller, stronger, and more powerful.

OVER-THE-SHOULDER:

This shot is a way of showing what is in front or behind a character, depending on which way it is used. It helps give the viewer a useful vantage point to understand the scene.

ONCE YOU'VE THOUGHT ABOUT THE SHOTS YOU WANT TO USE, YOU CAN MOVE YOUR SCRIPT ON TO THE 'SHOOTING SCRIPT' STAGE.

PLANNING YOUR SHOTS

Now that you know the lingo, we can begin breaking down the script into shots. This forms what is called a shooting script. The script tells the story and gives the actors their lines. The shooting script becomes a checklist and guide to all of the shots that you need to film for each scene. To learn how to do it, let's go back to the example script from page 12 and break it down into shots.

THE SHOOTING SCRIPT IS A COMPANION GUIDE TO YOUR SCRIPT. YOU'LL USE BOTH TOGETHER WHEN FILMING YOUR PROJECT.

Shot 1

The scene starts with a boy exploring a cellar. The scene is supposed to be mysterious and a little bit creepy, so we have to get that across to the audience with our choice of shots.

Shot 1 needs to tell us:
• Location
• Characters present
• Tone of the scene

How to do it:
I'd suggest using a long shot of the boy exploring the cellar, shot from behind a pile of old furniture at the back of the room. This clearly explains where we are (a cellar) and who is in the scene (the boy).

HANDY TIP!
You can shoot this so that the camera will be peering at the character from behind a pile of old furniture, as if the boy is being watched. This should make it feel a bit creepy.

Shot 2 needs to tell us:
- More information about the character
- That there is a shimmering light
- That the boy notices the shimmering light

How to do it:
I would move into a medium close-up of the boy as he looks around the room. I would have a crew member reflect a light from a shiny surface over his face after a few seconds and have the boy react to it, looking towards the source of the light off-camera.

Shot 3 needs to tell us:
Where exactly is the light coming from?

How to do it:
I would quickly cut to an over-the-shoulder shot of the boy walking towards the source of the shimmering light. At this point the viewer would notice that the light is coming from the same location that Shot 1 was taken from.

Shots 2 and 3

Next, the scene has the boy notice a shimmering light coming from the end of the room. Let's do this in two parts.

Shot 4

The scene continues as the boy approaches the light and an expression of astonishment begins to appear on his face as the light source illuminates it. The boy also delivers two lines of dialogue.

Shot 4 needs to tell us:
- The boy is astonished at what he has found
- The boy has two lines of dialogue

How to do it:
I would go back to the framing of Shot 2 but follow the boy as he approaches the light by moving the camera backwards. I can capture his performance to show his astonishment and clearly show his face, helping to make the line of dialogue easier to understand.

THE SHOOTING SCRIPT

Once you've written your scene and broken it down into shots, you've got the building blocks of that part of the story completed. The final thing to do is to put the information into an easy-to-read table that you and your crew can use as the checklist during filming. This is your shooting script. You could also draw a basic plan of the set.

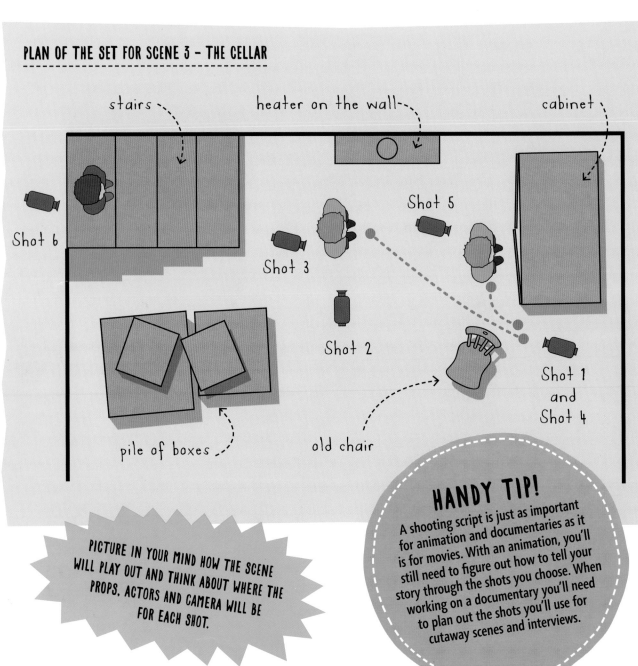

PLAN OF THE SET FOR SCENE 3 – THE CELLAR

stairs

heater on the wall

cabinet

Shot 6

Shot 5

Shot 3

Shot 2

Shot 1 and Shot 4

pile of boxes

old chair

PICTURE IN YOUR MIND HOW THE SCENE WILL PLAY OUT AND THINK ABOUT WHERE THE PROPS, ACTORS AND CAMERA WILL BE FOR EACH SHOT.

HANDY TIP!

A shooting script is just as important for animation and documentaries as it is for movies. With an animation, you'll still need to figure out how to tell your story through the shots you choose. When working on a documentary you'll need to plan out the shots you'll use for cutaway scenes and interviews.

What number is the scene within the story? Think of these like chapters in a book. Scene 1 is the first and is followed by scene 2, and so on.

The 'Action' column summarises what we need to know: shot type, physical actions on screen, characters present, angles, is dialogue delivered?

Scene No.	Shot No.	Action	Dialogue	Checklist
3	1	Long shot: the boy explores the cellar, shot from behind a pile of old furniture.	N	√
3	2	Medium close-up: the boy looks around the room. A shimmering light appears across his face. He notices and looks towards the source.	N	√
3	3	Over-the-shoulder: the boy looks towards a pile of old furniture. A dim light source can be seen from behind a few objects.	N	√
3	4	Medium close-up following the boy as he approaches the light source, astonished, and delivers lines.	Y	√
3	5	Over-the-shoulder as the boy hears footsteps and quickly puts the object inside the cabinet. We do not see the object.	N	√
3	6	Over-the-shoulder (reversed): the boy spins around on his heels as Mother enters the scene at the top of the stairway and delivers lines.	Y	
3	7	(Optional) close-up shot of the cabinet, with the camera moving in closer as we hear the characters leave the scene and the lights go out.	N	

It's useful to see at a glance (by noting 'Y' for 'yes' and 'N' for 'no') if there is dialogue in the shot. This way you can make sure you've definitely captured all of the dialogue for the scene.

Leave an empty column on your table for you to check off once each shot has been completed. This is really your 'shopping list' for the day when you are filming.

What number shot are we talking about?

SINCE WE ALREADY KNOW THE ARTISTIC REASONS OF WHY WE ARE DOING EACH SHOT, WE DON'T ACTUALLY NEED TO ADD IT HERE. WE JUST NEED THE FACTS.

TRY IT OUT

Now it's your turn to give it a go and turn your own script into a shooting script. You can try making up your own version of shots for this example scene if you want to have a practice first. Remember to make sure that each shot is there for a purpose.

VISUALISE EVERY SHOT

We've got our idea into a script and now we even have a list of planned shots to tell our story. We're almost there now! We'll soon be at the point every filmmaker dreams of, when the project is finally ready to shoot. You often see film directors using their hands to frame an imaginary shot. No matter what shape your set is, the finished shot will be a rectangle. Only part of what you see with your eyes when you watch your actors on set will actually appear in the film. You need to plan in advance how you are going to frame each shot, so that the composition is clear and attractive.

STORYBOARDS

A storyboard is a visual diagram of each shot to help the cast and crew picture the scene for recording. They can really help in this regard, and a well-crafted storyboard is a great addition to your shooting script. However, they can take a very long time to complete. They are also only useful if you are able to quickly and accurately draw the shots from your imagination. Unfortunately, without the right training, most of us can't.

'WOW' FACTOR!

A WELL-DRAWN STORYBOARD CAN LOOK LIKE A GRAPHIC NOVEL STYLE VERSION OF THE FILM, JUST WITH NO SPEECH BUBBLES.

KEY DIAGRAMS

I think key diagrams are more useful than a storyboard, and they aren't too time-consuming. For example, if my artistic skills are limited to stick figures, I won't spend my time drawing a detailed storyboard unless the shot is very complicated and a diagram will be needed.

STORYBOARDS CAN BE EITHER THE MOST VALUABLE PIECE OF PRODUCTION PLANNING, OR A WASTE OF TIME. IT'S WONDERFUL WHEN THEY'RE USEFUL, BUT NOT WHEN THEY TAKE UP MORE TIME THAN THEY'RE WORTH.

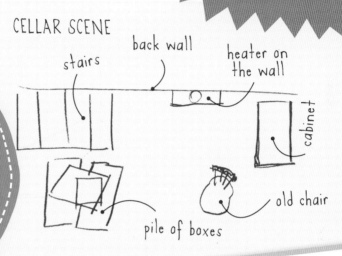

CELLAR SCENE

stairs — back wall — heater on the wall — cabinet — old chair — pile of boxes

HANDY TIP!

Drawing some practical shooting diagrams can be a great idea. I often make an overhead plan to show where actors and cameras will be moving in a shot, to help people get the idea of how the scene plays out.

ANIMATION

Animation is one type of filmmaking where you really can't get away with not having a general visual plan for the project. All of the visuals are created artistically, by making models, sets and drawings. Even if you're not a great artist, it does make sense to sketch up some 'thumbnail images' (very quick, small pictures) that give an idea of how each shot will look. Even stick figures will work in this type of project; anything that helps to keep you on track with each shot is valuable.

Once you've made yourself a storyboard or key diagram, ask yourself these questions:

• Can you easily see the different characters?

• Do your shots clearly show who is speaking and who they are speaking to?

• Do your shots clearly show what is unfolding in your story?

• Do they get across the mood you are trying to achieve?

• From your planned shots, could you draw a map of what the location looks like and where the characters start and end the scene?

THE 180° RULE

At this stage, it's good to take a step back and just check that what you're doing works. Will it look as good as it can by shooting it this way, and will the audience understand what is going on? Play back the scene in your mind as you intend to film it from the shooting script.

The last question on the checklist on page 21 is a tricky one, and if the answer is 'no', then your audience might feel lost. These questions relate to a key filmmaking tactic called the 180° rule. It is the main reason why scenes can sometimes be difficult to follow. Getting it right immediately makes your film look and feel more professional.

An example

If we have two characters talking to each other we might have three shots that we continually cut back and forth between.

HOW IT WORKS

Characters and their movements on screen should have a linear motion throughout the scene. If they begin the scene facing or moving in one direction, they should continue to face or move in that direction, otherwise it becomes confusing.

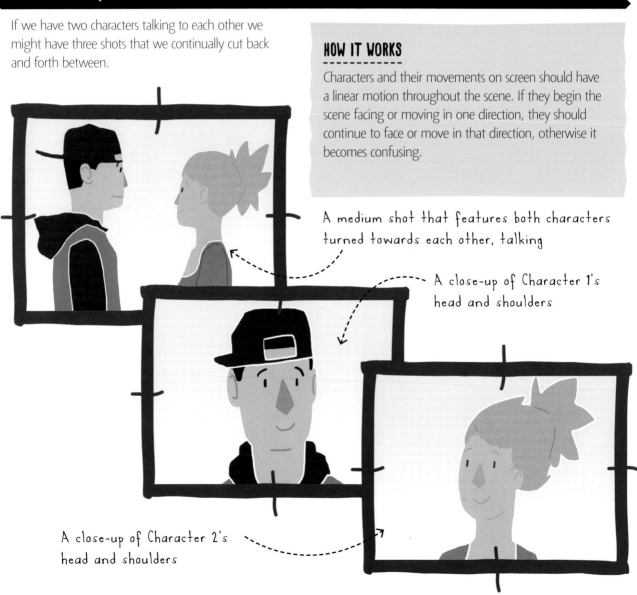

A medium shot that features both characters turned towards each other, talking

A close-up of Character 1's head and shoulders

A close-up of Character 2's head and shoulders

WHY DOES IT WORK?

The reason that this scene looks good is that the characters appear to be looking at each other, even when the other character is not in shot. Their conversation seems natural. If we were to all of a sudden shoot from the other side of the room, so that they were facing the other way, it would break the 180° rule.

Keep the camera on one side

HOW TO DO IT

Imagine you're looking straight at a friend who is looking back at you. Visualise a line on the floor that goes from your feet to theirs, with a camera placed on your left, looking towards the two of you having a conversation. You could then move the camera anywhere on that side of the line and it would not appear odd.

However, if you were to put the camera on the other side of the line and point it towards you, on screen you and your friend would appear to have switched places. This is very confusing to the viewer, which is why it is almost never done by professionals.

HANDY TIP!

When imagining your shots, try to visualise where you will be putting your camera. Do you switch sides at any time? If you do, would it be confusing? Sometimes it won't, but most times it will, so it's worth having a look at your scenes just to check.

WHEN YOU GET IT RIGHT:

- The film feels more professional
- The audience don't get confused
- The audience can follow the events of the story by imagining the space your film takes place in.

MAKING EVERY SHOT COUNT

We've spoken about production value before – it's the professional quality that the film appears to have. The way you film each shot can have a huge impact on this. Get it right, and the film looks amazing.

Let's say that I'm shooting a scene that has some action and dialogue in it. The action and dialogue are supposed to be very powerful and show a great deal of emotion. In an ideal world I would like to cast an award-winning actor or actress for the part. But I only have access to some friends who do not have that type of experience. What do I do?

Choices

1. Rather than show the actor not giving the performance I would like, I could remove the scene. But it's likely that this will affect the storyline.

2. I could accept the level of my actor's abilities and tell the story the way I had originally planned. However, it might not look very professional.

3. I could tell the story in a different way to minimise the acting issues and maximise the production value.

SOLVING THE PROBLEM

Let's say, for example, that the scene was a very emotional conversation between two characters over the phone. Rather than see both characters delivering their lines into a phone, you could simplify it.

HANDY TIP!
With the right perspective on a scene, you can easily turn a negative into a positive with just a few tweaks. Be creative with your shots to maximise your production value.

Solutions

1 I could shoot it so that the audience sees one character but only hears the other. We can't always detect acting quality so well by voice alone.

TRY TO IMAGINE OTHER SCENES THAT THIS TECHNIQUE COULD WORK IN.

2 Another option is to have the camera slowly creep towards the other character from behind. This way we won't see his face, which is where most emotion is shown. Instead, the viewer has to use her imagination and build the picture in her head. Audiences typically do this with the best memories they have of similar scenes. The camera movement also adds importance to the character it moves towards, directing the audience's attention to him. Suddenly the problem we had has now turned into the best shot in the scene.

GOOD ENOUGH FOR THE TRAILER?

Now we're getting somewhere! The next step is to ask one final question about each shot before we set them in stone: is this shot good enough for the trailer? This question is really important because if you can answer 'yes' to it for every shot in your film, you will be on track to make a visual masterpiece. What you are doing is evaluating the shot and deciding whether or not there is a better way to shoot it. If not, then we're good to go.

'WOW' FACTOR!

NEXT TIME YOU'RE AT THE CINEMA, STUDY THE TRAILERS. BIG STUDIOS ONLY USE THEIR BEST SHOTS FOR THE TRAILER.

PLAN, PLAN, PLAN!

Now we're ready to move into the production stage. Starting with a basic idea, you've developed it into a script, broken it down into sensible, bite-sized scenes, and planned all your shots. Each shot has been checked and double-checked, meaning that by now you've really spent the time to make this film as good as it can possibly be. You're ready to start filming.

ORGANISING YOUR FILMING SESSIONS

You don't need to film your scenes in the order that they will appear in the film. For example, your script might call for the opening and closing scenes to be filmed at the main character's house, with other scenes at different locations in between. It would make sense to film all the scenes at the house in the same session before moving on to a different location.

It might be possible to shoot your entire film in one day, but it's likely that you'll need a few separate filming dates to record everything you need. You need to plan each day's filming carefully, so that you make the most of your time. Anticipating any possible problems can help things run more smoothly on the day.

> TAKE A MOMENT TO THINK ABOUT WHAT YOU'VE DONE SO FAR. IT REALLY IS QUITE AN ACHIEVEMENT! THE HARD WORK YOU'VE PUT IN WILL MAKE YOUR FILM SOMETHING TO BE PROUD OF.

BUDGET

It doesn't matter how much or how little money you have to spend on the project, you still need to make a budget. If you begin shooting and then realise that you don't have enough money, you won't be able to complete your film. By budgeting, you can figure out what you already have, what you need, how to get it, and whether to adapt it if you can't get it.

What I need:

LOCATIONS
PROPS
CAST
COSTUMES

Crew and equipment list:

DIRECTOR
CAMERA OPERATOR
RUNNER (HELPER)
CAMERA

HANDY TIP!
You should try to get all of your shooting dates planned out before you start, but if this is not possible for whatever reason, then go ahead and start filming once your first day is planned.

Read through your script and list everything that is featured in the story. This includes everything that will appear in the finished film.

After you have the story elements, list the equipment and crew you will need. Some of these might not be needed for your project, but others will.

EVEN IF YOUR ACTORS ARE FRIENDS WHO DON'T EXPECT TO BE PAID, THE LEAST YOU CAN DO IS TO PROVIDE THEM WITH LUNCH AND SNACKS. FILMING CAN BE HUNGRY WORK!

WHAT ELSE DO I NEED?

There are a few things you might not have thought of that need to be included in your budget. For example, how are you going to travel to your locations? And you will need to provide food and drinks for your cast and crew.

Think about how much all of these things will cost. Most of them will be free, but others won't. Add up all the costs and see if you can still afford it. If you can, great!

GETTING THE TEAM TOGETHER

You've now got a list of all of the items that you'll need to organise for your shooting dates. By working through the list, your next job is to source your crew, locations, actors, props, costumes and equipment. Your best option is usually to ask friends to help you. They can be your crew and cast.

PRODUCTION MEETINGS

Once you have all of these elements in place, the most important thing to do is to meet with everyone involved to discuss the project and get everyone up to speed. Professional film crews always hold production meetings before filming starts, so that everyone involved knows what they are expected to do.

HANDY TIP!

Your friends might be able to help with locations and props, too. Maybe they have access to a sports hall, or their mum's workplace could serve as an interesting location. It never hurts to ask!

Production Meeting Agenda

- Pass out copies of the script

- Discuss the story and talk everyone through what it is you're trying to create

- Check dates and times that everyone can make

- Make a shooting schedule

- Arrange travel to the filming locations

- Assign responsibility for props and costumes

- Make back-up plans (e.g. an alternate day for outdoor shoots, in case the weather is bad)

When you conduct your first meeting, you'll want to be well prepared in order to get lots of things organised. You should create a list of all the topics you want to discuss and have it with you to prompt you during the meeting.

MEETING MINUTES

Give a copy of the notes to everyone after the meeting has finished so that they can all be aware of the plans. At this point you should be well prepared to finalise your filming plans and can book dates and times to get the filming completed.

HANDY TIP!
Ask one of your friends to take notes during the meeting, and to record all the decisions that are made. You might be too busy leading the meeting to get everything written down.

READY TO SHOOT!

From this point we will move into practical ways to help you develop your filming and directing skills in preparation for your filming dates. These will be the skills you need to make the best use of the time you have booked to create your film. If you use your time well and master the techniques in the next few chapters, you will end up with the best film that you possibly can.

CAMERA WORK

The most important piece of equipment for a filmmaker is obviously the camera. Cameras are complex pieces of technology, and understanding them fully can take years of study and practice. However, there are some basic things that every filmmaker should know when it comes to how they work.

The camera

Video cameras range from the tiny versions built into smartphones, through the small hand-held cameras your parents use to record your school play, and up to the large cameras used by professionals and costing thousands of pounds. But every single type of video camera consists of two main parts: the lens and the body.

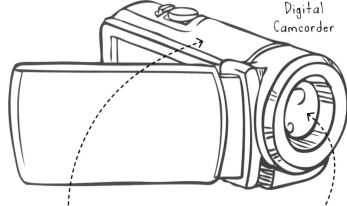

Digital Camcorder

Compact Digital Camera

The body of the camera contains the hardware that turns the light into the digital image you see as the final result.

The lens is the part of the camera that lets light in and focuses it into an image.

Smartphone

Digital SLR Camera

GETTING THE BEST OUT OF YOUR CAMERA

This is a very simplified notion of how a camera works, but it is important for one crucial reason. Your job as a filmmaker is to put the best quality of content into the lens so that the body (or computer side) of the camera has less work to do.

The cameras that are built into smartphones or digital cameras and camcorders are often used to record special occasions. The videos try to capture everything that is around them as clearly as possible in order to best capture the memory.

This means that the computer part of the camera actively lightens areas that it feels it needs to in order to best capture the scene, giving you very little control over the final image. As a director, you want control over the image to tell the story in your own way. You'll need to control the lighting as well as you can by choosing locations carefully and making the best use of the available lighting.

'WOW' FACTOR!

A MODERN CAMERA IS AN AMAZING TOOL, BUT IT CAN'T WORK MAGIC. WHAT YOU PUT INTO IT IS MORE OR LESS WHAT YOU GET OUT. EVEN THE MOST EXPENSIVE CAMERA CAN'T HIDE A POOR PERFORMANCE, A BADLY DESIGNED SET OR AN AWKWARDLY FRAMED SHOT.

YOUR JOB AS A DIRECTOR IS BATTLING FOR CONTROL OVER THE IMAGE FROM HERE ON OUT.

HANDY TIP!
Where possible, you should avoid extreme light situations (too dark or too bright), as the camera's computer will kick in and try to adapt the image too much.

FILM OR DIGITAL VIDEO?

For over 100 years, nearly all Hollywood movies were shot on film, but these days many are shot in digital video instead. Even the movies that are still shot on film are often sent to cinemas digitally to be screened. The main reason for this is money. It costs about £900 to print and send just one copy of a film to a cinema. Doing it digitally is much cheaper.

MOVING SHOTS

Now that you know the basics about cameras, let's talk about shots. We've discussed what certain shots look like and how you go about creating them, but the ones you've looked at so far are all static shots. This means that the camera doesn't move. To make your film look more interesting – and more professional – you'll need to get your camera moving. There are three main ways to do this.

Shot 1: THE PAN

WHAT IT IS: Panning is what we call the camera motion when we move horizontally across a scene.

HOW TO DO IT: If you were to stand still and film a scene, while carefully moving the camera from left to right, you would be panning through the scene. You can also use this technique to pan in time with a character's movements to better follow them through the scene.

THE EFFECT: This shot gives a little more detail about the setting that the scene takes place in than a static (non-moving) shot.

HANDHELD OR TRIPOD: Either, so long as the camera operator stays stationary and simply turns the camera left to right or vice versa.

Shot 2: THE TILT

WHAT IT IS: Tilting is simply the vertical version of panning.

HOW TO DO IT: The camera operator stays stationary whilst the camera is tilted up and down towards the sky or ground.

THE EFFECT: This shot is most notably used in creating high and low angle shots.

HANDHELD OR TRIPOD: Either is fine.

Shot 3: THE ZOOM

WHAT IT IS: A zoom is when the image appears to become larger or smaller, depending on whether the camera is zooming in or out.

HOW TO DO IT: This is a feature built into all video cameras. The camera is held in one position during the zoom.

THE EFFECT: This technique can be used to show the importance of an event or item, and to help guide the viewer's attention.

HANDHELD OR TRIPOD: Either, though it works best when the camera is held very steady, such as on a tripod.

'WOW' FACTOR!

MANY STUNTS ARE FILMED BY MOVING THE CAMERA VERY FAR AWAY FROM THE ACTOR AND ZOOMING ALL THE WAY IN. THIS MAKES THE ACTOR LOOK MUCH CLOSER TO THE BACKGROUND THAN THEY ACTUALLY ARE. EXPLOSIONS AND CAR CHASES CAN THEN BE FILMED A SAFE DISTANCE FROM THE ACTOR BUT APPEAR TO BE VERY CLOSE TO THEM ON SCREEN.

SOME CAMERAS HAVE FISHEYE MODES WHICH ALLOW THEM TO ZOOM OUT TO ULTRA-WIDE SETTINGS, RESULTING IN A DISTORTED CIRCULAR IMAGE.

ADVANCED ZOOMING

By zooming into an image you distort its shape slightly. When fully zoomed out, the edges of your image can be a little bit circular. When you zoom in you remove this circular effect and flatten the image. In a nutshell, you make the background look bigger when zooming out and smaller when zooming in. You can use this to set up interesting shots.

MORE COMPLEX SHOTS

When you watch movies, you'll notice that the camera is almost always moving in some way or another. The movements are controlled and smooth, giving the shot a very professional look. You, too, can achieve shots like these to make your movie look great. As before, you'll want to practise the camera work before recording each shot – but with a little work you'll be ready to call 'action!'

Shot 4: THE DOLLY SHOT

WHAT IT IS: A dolly shot is used to make the camera appear to glide through the scene without resistance. It can be used to move the camera forward, backwards, side-to-side or diagonally.

HOW TO DO IT: Filmmakers achieve this effect by having the camera mounted on a large skateboard-like surface that is connected to a smooth metal track on the floor.

THE EFFECT: This type of shot always looks nicer than a zoom or a pan because the audience actually feel as though they are within the scene.

HANDY TIP!

You can create a dolly effect by filming whilst sitting on a computer or office chair with wheels and having a friend slowly move you through the scene. Be careful to keep the motion as smooth as possible.

1 Sitting on a wheelie chair, position yourself at the start of the scene.

2 Get a friend to slowly move you through the scene while you film.

3 With a smooth motion, you can pan across a wide area.

Shot 5: THE TRACKING SHOT

WHAT IT IS: A tracking shot is a type of dolly shot in which the camera follows a character while he or she moves through a scene. It can also follow an object such as a car.

HOW TO DO IT: Filmmakers either use a dolly track to follow the actor as he moves, or a camera held by the operator as he or she walks along.

THE EFFECT: The character appears stationary in the frame while the background moves, giving the impression of urgent motion.

Shot 6: THE DOLLY ZOOM

WHAT IT IS: The dolly zoom or 'contra-zoom' is a technique for making the background of a scene become massively distorted, by either shrinking or expanding it whilst the actor stays the same size.

HOW TO DO IT: You move the camera towards or away from your actor using the dolly technique and adjust the zoom on the camera at the same time. This keeps the actor appearing the same size on screen.

THE EFFECT: The dolly zoom is a great way to get your audience to understand that something important has happened. It results in a really interesting video effect that you've probably seen in many films before.

FILMING A PERFECT DOLLY ZOOM TAKES A LOT OF PRACTICE AND CAREFUL TIMING. BUT IT CAN BE GREAT IN EITHER LIVE ACTION OR STOP-MOTION ANIMATION.

1 Set up your shot, paying close attention to the framing of your subject.

2 As you move the camera away from your actor, zoom in to keep your subject the same size and position that they were in step 1.

HANDHELD OR TRIPOD?

One thing to think about when shooting is whether to film handheld or use a tripod. The tripod will give you a stable image, and this can be great for shots where there is a lot of detail for the viewer to take in. On the other hand, handheld shots give a more human feel, but you do need to be careful that you do not cause too much camera shake whilst filming.

REASONS FOR USING CONTROLLED HANDHELD:

- The slight motion adds a human feel to the shot.
- We can cover the scene in one take by moving the camera.
- We can achieve movements not possible on a tripod or dolly.

CONTROLLED HANDHELD

There is a middle ground between handheld and tripod shots, and it's called 'controlled handheld'. Sometimes you want the shot to look a little bit unpolished without it being obviously handheld, like you would expect from a found-footage movie.

HANDY TIP!

When filming stop-motion animation, each photo you take needs to be as close to the previous one as possible for a smooth effect. It is probably a good idea to use a tripod for this type of film, as you'll have far more control over the camera.

HOW TO MAKE YOUR HANDHELD SHOTS LOOK GREAT:

- Keep your shoulders and elbows up and to the sides.
- Hold the camera gently with your hands and allow your wrists to relax. If you're tense, you'll shake the camera.
- When you move the camera, try to move only your shoulders and elbows. This gives you smoother, more controlled movements on screen.

BECOMING BETTER AT HANDHELD WORK TAKES A LOT OF TIME AND PRACTICE.

RIGGING

So now you've got the shots down, let's look at tools that can make them even better. In the industry they use professional equipment (called 'rigging'), such as dolly and track systems, cranes, camera stabilisers and a whole load of very useful but very expensive gadgets.

No budget? Don't worry: you don't need professional equipment. All these bits of expensive kit are just tools to help get the job done. With practice and a few homemade tools of your own, you can achieve the same effect – and I'll show you ways that we can actually do it better.

MAKING YOUR OWN RIG

Chances are the device you're using to make your movie is quite small - probably a smartphone or camcorder. Professional movie cameras are big! Camera technology has advanced so much that they don't need to be so big anymore, but they keep them this way because big cameras are easier to control when doing handheld work. However, we can easily adapt our smaller cameras to do the same, and on the next page I'll show you how.

'WOW' FACTOR!

WHERE POSSIBLE, WALK BACKWARDS WHILST FILMING CONTROLLED HANDHELD. IT SOUNDS ODD, BUT YOU'LL HAVE MORE CONTROL! JUST BE CAREFUL NOT TO TRIP OVER ANYTHING AND BE AWARE OF YOUR SURROUNDINGS. MOONWALKING IS OPTIONAL!

It's easy to trip or fall over an object when filming if you're not looking where you're going. Plan your movements ahead of time, clear a walkway in preparation for filming, and have someone on set to keep an eye on your path, ready to stop you if you're about to cause a disaster.

MAKING A SMARTPHONE STABILISER

This method is best suited for smartphones, but can easily be adapted to other types of cameras. This rig is simple to make, and even easier to put together if you have a friend to help.

WHAT YOU NEED:

- A smartphone
- A spare hard plastic case for the smartphone
- A central column (can be anything long and straight, such as a broom handle)
- A suitable strong adhesive, such as duct tape, a hot glue gun, or super glue
- A counterweight, such as a small bag filled with marbles, nuts and bolts, or coins

'WOW' FACTOR!

WITH THIS RIG YOU CAN FRAME UP A SHOT WORTHY OF A HOLLYWOOD FILM! BUT YOU CAN ALSO GET SHOTS THAT HOLLYWOOD CAN'T, BY TAKING YOUR CAMERA OFF THE RIG AND GETTING INTO SMALLER LOCATIONS THAT THEIR BULKY CAMERAS WON'T FIT INTO. YOU CAN SHOOT INTERESTING ANGLES SUCH AS A POINT OF VIEW FROM A CAR BOOT, UNDER A BED OR INSIDE A CUPBOARD.

Step 1

Secure the central column to the back of the smartphone case at one end, leaving about 5 centimetres at the top and making sure the smartphone case is in a landscape orientation. Make sure that the join is very strong.

smartphone case

HANDY TIP!

There are countless DIY rig instructions available on the internet that might better suit your camera and the equipment you have available. It's worth checking these out.

Step 2

Attach the counterweight bag to the other end of the central column, secured well so that the bag is not able to swing while the camera is moving. You will need to be able to add and remove weight from the bag in order to balance it better.

ADHESIVES CAN BE DANGEROUS WHEN USED INCORRECTLY, SO BE CAREFUL AND GET AN ADULT TO HELP YOU.

central column

counterweight

Step 3

Hold the central column with both hands spaced apart at least 15 centimetres and find a position that is comfortable for each hand. Wrap a few layers of duct tape around the central column at these points. This will help you easily identify the holding points and improve your grip.

Step 4

Once you have checked that each join is tightly secured, mount your camera onto the rig by putting it into the smartphone case. Balance the rig on your hand by holding it in the centre at a 90° angle. Adjust the counterweight, by adding or removing weight, until it balances the camera. Once the rig is balanced, it will make the camera easy to control in smooth motions.

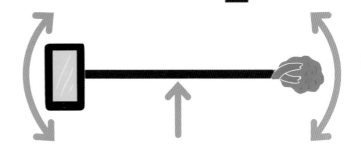

Step 5

Try to create some floating handheld shots with your new rig. It should be much easier, as you now have a larger surface area to control the camera movement. What's more, the camera is now counterbalanced by the weight at the bottom.

HANDY TIP!
Before you start filming, practise the skills you've learned in this chapter. Go around the house and film anything you like, making sure to plan your shots carefully. Work on each technique until you can do it easily, either handheld or with a tripod.

LIGHTING AND SOUND

It's easy to get so focused on things like scripts, costumes and camera moves that you forget about two key aspects of your film: lighting and sound. In fact, lighting is key to setting the scene when you are filming. Not only does it add depth and emotion to your image, but your shots also seem more professional if you've controlled the lighting.

Lighting is both complicated and expensive, so you probably won't have all the necessary equipment to do it the same way as the professionals do. However, there are some DIY methods that you can use without spending any money.

3-POINT LIGHTING

First, let's have a look at some basic lighting techniques. The most common form of lighting is known as 3-point lighting and it is used in most films in one way or another. Its effect is created by using three light sources. This technique allows you to add depth to your image and direct the audience to the important parts of the scene.

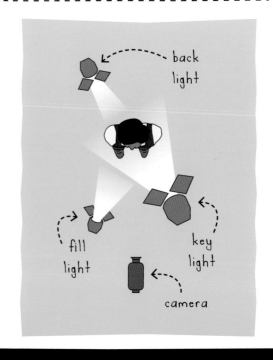

back light

fill light

key light

camera

ASK ANY PROFESSIONAL FILMMAKER WHAT AREA IS MOST OVERLOOKED BY FIRST-TIME DIRECTORS, AND THEY'LL PROBABLY SAY IT'S LIGHTING AND SOUND.

Light 1: THE KEY LIGHT

The first light source is known as the key light. It is the strongest light source within the image and forms the major illumination within the scene.

The key light is usually positioned high and to one side.

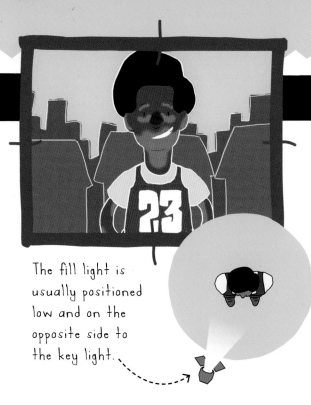

Light 2: THE FILL LIGHT

The fill light is weaker and more diffused, dimly illuminating the shadow areas of your scene caused by the key light. It allows you to create depth and contrast in the image without letting any one area get too dark. Using the fill light in this way leads to an interesting image with a balanced sense of contrast.

The fill light is usually positioned low and on the opposite side to the key light.

'WOW' FACTOR!

A FILL LIGHT SOFTENS ANY SHADOWS PRODUCED BY THE KEY LIGHT. WITHOUT A FILL LIGHT, YOUR ACTORS' FACES MAY HAVE HARSH SHADOWS.

Light 3: THE BACK LIGHT

The back light is used to add a great sense of depth to the image. It typically illuminates the scene from behind, pointing more or less towards the camera (but out of sight of the lens). This illuminates the rear edges of the people and objects in the scene, making them stand out from the background.

The back light is usually positioned at about head height and on the opposite side to the key light.

USING AVAILABLE LIGHT

The 3-point lighting system is great for studios, where you have all the equipment you need. When you think about lighting your own scenes, the first thing to do is to recognise what is available to help light the location.

Whilst shooting in the day, if you're in an inside location, chances are you'll have lights or lamps available to use, and can adapt them to create your composition. If you're outside, the sun will be the main light source.

HANDY TIP!

If you're shooting outdoors, not only will you have natural light to take into account, but remember that you'll be unlikely to have electrical power available.

LIGHTING INTERIOR SCENES

When shooting an interior scene, the daylight coming in from the windows will be the strongest light source, so it makes a good key light. We can use lamps to dimly illuminate the shadowed areas to give us some nice subtle contrast. Finally, we can use the ceiling lights to form the backlight in the scene and give us depth.

LIGHTING EXTERIOR SCENES

For an exterior shot we'll probably have to be more creative. If we can find a large bright surface we can position it near our characters to bounce the natural light in the opposite direction and act as a fill light. The same technique can also be used to illuminate the back of the characters, giving us more depth in the image.

HANDY TIP!

All cameras react differently to dark situations, so you'll have to do some practice shoots to see how your camera copes.

NIGHT-TIME SHOOTING

In some ways, shooting at night can be very easy – at least for indoor scenes. If it's dark outside, you'll have more control over the lighting of a scene by manipulating lights and lamps within your location.

However, outdoor night shoots can be very difficult to get right. There is no correct answer for this type of situation, so you'll have to experiment with bouncing light around from different sources such as the moon, streetlights and even torches.

DIY REFLECTOR BOARD

In order to bounce all of that light you'll need some reflector boards to help get the job done. You can easily make these at home by recycling old boxes.

WHAT YOU'LL NEED:

- Large panels of card from old boxes (the bigger the better)
- Sticky tape
- Aluminium foil

1 Take your box and cut out a large square or rectangular panel.

2 Cut strips from the remainder of the box and reinforce the edges of your card panel on one side.

3 Take sheets of aluminium foil and lightly crumple them. Be careful not to rip the foil or stress it too much.

4 Carefully unfold the foil. It should now have a lightly crumpled texture - this will be used to reflect diffused light.

5 Use sticky tape to secure the aluminium sheet to the card panel on the non-reinforced side. Add more sheets if you need to until the panel is completely covered.

'WOW' FACTOR!

WITH MORE REFLECTOR BOARDS ON LOCATION YOU CAN CREATE SOME FAIRLY ELABORATE LIGHTING SCENARIOS BY JUST USING AVAILABLE LIGHT.

USING THE REFLECTOR BOARD

Get one of your crew to angle the board towards the light source and the character at the same time. Adjust the distance to make the effect more or less pronounced. The closer you put the reflector board to the character, the brighter the reflected light will be.

RECORDING AUDIO

Audio is another area that is often overlooked, but you must get it right to keep the audience engrossed. We'll happily watch a movie such as a found-footage film where the visuals are intentionally all over the place, but if you were watching a movie and the sound kept cutting in and out, you would turn it off.

It's unlikely that you'll have access to professional audio equipment, but that doesn't matter: we can make the best of what we've got. Here are a few tips.

Tip 1: CHOOSE THE RIGHT LOCATION

The types of camera you'll be using will pick up background noise. We need to minimise that noise by picking the locations that will offer the least amount of noise pollution. The best places are either interior locations where you can close the nearby doors and windows to minimise the background noise, or exterior locations where people are not constantly walking by.

HANDY TIP!

When you're filming, your crew must stay perfectly silent to avoid ruining the take. Modern video cameras are designed to pick up almost any sound within the immediate area.

Tip 2: DEADEN THE SOUND

Raid your house for blankets, duvets and towels, and lay them across large flat surfaces within your location. Just as light can bounce, sound bounces too. By putting thick cloth over large flat surfaces you remove their ability to bounce noises around your set.

THIS WORKS BEST INSIDE BUT IT CAN ALSO HAVE AN EFFECT IN CERTAIN OUTDOOR LOCATIONS. MAKE SURE YOUR CLOTHES ARE NOT IN SHOT!

Tip 3: THE WILD TRACK

When you edit your film, you'll probably be cutting and moving clips around to speed up or drag out each scene. Every time you cut you'll be able to hear the background noise cutting in as you put the clips next to each other. To fix this, filmmakers layer what is known as a 'wild track' over the audio. To create a wild track you simply record the natural sound of a location on your camera whilst everyone is being silent for a minute or so. This gives you some background noise that is specific to the location, which you can use to hide your edit points.

Tip 4: AUDIO FOR INTERVIEWS

With documentary interviews you need your subject's answers to be as clear as possible. Try and stay completely silent whilst listening to their responses in order to keep the audio track clean. This can feel very strange to begin with, but it makes a real difference.

Tip 5: RECORD THE DIALOGUE LATER

Sometimes the audio in the location is just going to be impossible to use. If you really can't get the scene in any other way you might opt to re-record the audio at a different location (at home, for example) after you have recorded the actual scenes. This will allow you to get cleaner audio, but can be tricky to get right.

BE A CONFIDENT DIRECTOR

To become a good director you need to believe in your ability to tell the story well. Much of what it takes to create a good film is completely in your head. It's really about being confident in your abilities and letting that confidence influence your film. There are a few tips I'd like to share which can help boost your confidence. These are all techniques I use when I'm filming – and they really affect the way I shoot on the day.

Tip 1: TASK DIRECTION

Sometimes your actors aren't really actors. Often they are your friends who have agreed to be in your film. Whilst they might be happy to help, they might not have any experience and therefore might not be able to perform the scene as you would like. This is something that happens quite a lot when you start making movies. The technique you can use to combat this is called 'task direction'.

Rather than give your actors lines to remember and act out, give them tasks to complete and let them improvise. You are still directing their behaviour, but they'll tackle the task independently and it will look less forced.

Here's an example: if you want to have a scene where a character argues over the price of skateboard repairs with the repair man, instead of having them memorise and perform the scene, give them each a suitable task.

You might tell the customer to pay for the repairs, but spend no more than £20. Separately tell the repair man to not take anything less than £40 for the repairs. The resulting conversation between the two actors may end up being more natural than the version in your script.

THIS TECHNIQUE IS INCREDIBLY USEFUL WHEN YOU'RE WORKING WITH INEXPERIENCED ACTORS.

Tip 2: MASTER SHOT

The next technique I like to use is really helpful and a great habit to get used to, and it's known as a master shot. Shooting a master shot means filming each scene from start to finish, without any breaks, from its widest shot. Once that's done, you'll shoot the close-ups and other shots planned in your shooting script. A master shot is incredibly useful because no matter what happens, we can still tell the story by using it. It's a filmmaker's safety net.

'WOW' FACTOR!

THE MASTER SHOT MAY SEEM UNUSUAL, BUT IT IS TRIED AND TESTED AND HAS BEEN USED IN SOME OF THE BEST SCENES IN HOLLYWOOD HISTORY.

HANDY TIP!
A master shot can save the day if filming gets disrupted for any reason. Maybe a key prop gets broken, it starts to rain or an actor has to leave.

Tip 3: CUTAWAYS

Cutaways are a great tool for any director. A cutaway is a standalone shot of an object or action within the scene. You can use them to cover up editing points in your video when you do not have a good enough visual for the planned shot. For example, maybe you only realise later that your actress has her eyes closed at a key moment. A cutaway lets you still use the audio from the take and tell the story, but to show something other than the characters in order to hide the mistake.

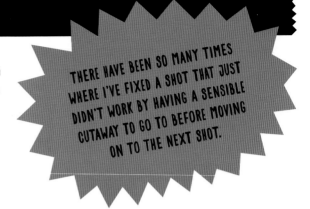

THERE HAVE BEEN SO MANY TIMES WHERE I'VE FIXED A SHOT THAT JUST DIDN'T WORK BY HAVING A SENSIBLE CUTAWAY TO GO TO BEFORE MOVING ON TO THE NEXT SHOT.

Tip 4: SHOW YOUR CONFIDENCE

Confidence really is key to becoming a good director. This often comes from experience, but even when starting your first project you can feel confident about knowing the techniques I've shown you. They can help you fix most situations you might find yourself in.

Being a confident director plays a big part in making a good film because your attitude has a knock-on effect on the whole project. By being and acting positive, you will have a positive effect on your film. If you are negative and lack confidence, chances are everyone else on your team will too.

- -

PRACTICE MAKES PERFECT

Becoming better at filmmaking won't happen over night. Your writing, camera, planning and leadership skills will naturally progress at their own rate, but it's better to grab any opportunity to improve on these as they come about. Next time you have to write a story of any kind, try to imagine it as a movie and write it in a cinematic way. If you're asked to record a video at a relative's birthday, turn it into a mini project to practice your technical skills. By thinking of the creative, planning and technical sides to filmmaking as separate elements, you'll see that they're all just as important as each other, each requiring practice and dedication to be mastered.

- If you feel confident on set, you look professional.

  ↓

- Your crew will respond to that and up their game to match your professionalism.

  ↓

- By working with a professional crew and having the filming go well, you will feel even more confident and professional.

  ↓

- When your actors see this, they will feel like they are working on something important.

  ↓

- They will feel more confident in the project and want to do a better job.

Getting Organised

When directing, you can end up with a lot of ideas zooming round your head, and it can be very difficult to process it all whilst trying to shoot your scenes. One of the simplest ways to keep yourself on track is to create an itinerary. This could be as simple as a list of the jobs you need to do on a filming day, with the time by which each task has to be completed. You can use this to make sure that everything gets done on schedule. Time your filming sessions and jot down any new shots and ideas that you get, fitting them in where time allows in order to stay focused, creative and - most importantly - sane!

HANDY TIP!

Take a quick look back at the goals you wrote down when you were working on Skill 1 (page 11). Have you completed any? Will they be completed during the filming process? Decide how you will now go about filming your project and hitting those targets at the same time.

FINAL WORD

Once you have filmed your project we will be moving on to the editing stage. But before you do that, have a look back at your footage and decide whether or not you are happy with it. Figure out what went well and what didn't, and decide whether or not you need to re-shoot anything.

EDITING YOUR FILM

In this section we are going to look at the technical side of finishing up your film. What you do in this stage of your production is likely to vary depending on what type of project you have made. If you've made a short film, music video or documentary as your project, then the next steps will involve selecting shots and retiming and reordering them to tell your story.

- -

GETTING YOUR VIDEOS ONTO THE COMPUTER

If you've made your film using a tablet, you might be better off using apps on the device to complete all of your editing. However, if you used a digital camera, camcorder or mobile phone, the first stage is to have a good look at what you've filmed on the device that you will be editing on.

It's usually very easy to get your footage onto a computer or tablet. Most of the time it's as simple as connecting up

the recording device to the computer with the supplied cable and dragging the footage from one to the other. Some devices supply their own software to assist in this process and will have their own tutorial on the subject. If you are really stuck, a quick search on the internet using the make and model of your recording device should help you to get to grips with it.

LOOK ONLINE FOR PHOTO OR VIDEO TUTORIALS. THEY ARE EASY TO FIND AND CAN BE A GREAT WAY TO VISUALLY UNDERSTAND THE EDITING PROCESS.

EDITING APPLICATIONS

After you have transferred your footage onto a computer or tablet, the next step is to figure out what software you will use to edit it. If you are using a Windows computer, you could use the Windows Live Movie Maker app made by Microsoft. Apple users can take advantage of iMovie which comes free with many of their computers or even Final Cut Pro – Apple's professional premium version of their editing software – if you have access to it.

Or you could search online for a free third-party app – there are many available for both Windows and Apple users.

Whichever application you use, there are normally plenty of instructional videos made by the developer and other users to help you create your film. Most programs take little more than a bit of experimentation to get to grips with.

EDITING SOFTWARE BASICS

There are four parts to an editing application:

DON'T BE AFRAID TO TRY OUT EDITING SOFTWARE. HAVE A PLAY AROUND, BUT REMEMBER TO SAVE A BACK-UP OF YOUR WORK REGULARLY!

The Monitor - A screen that shows what your edited videos in the timeline look like when played back.

The Clip Bin - Where all of your shots are stored ready to be used in your film.

HANDY TIP!
Apps can look quite different to each other, but they all have almost exactly the same workflow and basic design.

The Timeline - Where you place each of your clips, allowing you to reorder and cut down the videos to your liking in order to tell your story.

The Effects Panel - Where special effects that change the look and sound of your videos can be made along with transitions and titling options.

TABLET USERS

These same four parts to the editing process apply to tablets as well as computers and laptops, but the applications are usually designed to be more hands-on. Using a tablet's touch screen is a great way to quickly build your final film. Again, in-depth tutorials can be found with a quick internet search.

STOP MOTION

If you have created a stop-motion project, then you might have a few options available to you at this time. If you used an app to record your videos, you might be able to edit the shots directly from the very same app.

However, if you created a stop-motion film using a digital camera, or the app you used does not have editing capabilities, you will need to use another application to complete this stage of your film.

MAKING PROFESSIONAL EDITS

You are free to use any type of fancy transitions between your shots, but typically there are only two that are used in the industry. The most common technique is 'the cut', where one shot instantly jumps to the next. This tells the audience that the two shots happen continuously in time. Just make sure that each shot you cut between looks visually different enough from the last or you might end up with 'jump cuts'.

The next technique is 'the fade', whereby the first shot slowly fades away to reveal the next. This transition signifies some time has passed between the first and second shots.

It's worth knowing that there are also a selection of unusual transitions found in most video editing apps, such as wipes and peels. However, you'll probably very rarely use them.

Many transitions will work using both a cut or a fade. Play around to decide what is right for you and try to build sequences with variety. Throw in a fade once in a while and see if it works.

WORKING WITH AUDIO

Typically you'll have a few layers of audio in your edit. You'll likely have some kind of background music, maybe some ambient sound effects, followed by the audio that you recorded in the scene and finally small sections of your wild track (used to cover up where the audio might be slightly different between editing point). It's important to make the most of these layers to make your audience feel part of the story.

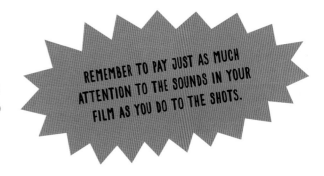

REMEMBER TO PAY JUST AS MUCH ATTENTION TO THE SOUNDS IN YOUR FILM AS YOU DO TO THE SHOTS.

SPECIAL EFFECTS

Many of the special-effects elements that are included in basic editing software are unlikely to be of much use. It's worth checking to see if there might be some effects that might be useful to telling your story. There could be some aged film effects that work well, or some distorting effects to play around with.

One area you'll almost always want to experiment with is the colour settings. With the colour correction effects you can change the tone of your image by adapting the colours. This can result in a better representation of the mood of the film. You could make dark and scary scenes veiled in shadows and blue/green tones like you would expect from a haunted house. Equally you could add a beautiful orange/golden tone to your film to simulate a romantic sunset scene. For each scene there are colours that will work better or worse, so experiment to decide what works best for your movie. Also look at other films with similar scenes and try to figure out what colours are more present in those sequences.

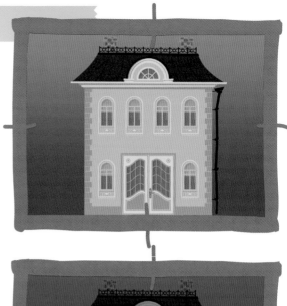

HANDY TIP!
Use these colouring techniques subtly so that they help the viewer identify the mood of the story, but do not distract from the film itself.

ADDING TITLES AND CREDITS

After the main part of your editing is complete, you'll probably want to add in some titles. Titles not only tell the audience the name of the film, but can be used to indicate where the film is taking place or give information about a person being interviewed in a documentary. When designing your titles, remember that the viewer should be able to read them easily so choose clear fonts and colours that contrast with the background.

You'll want a font that reflects the style or genre of your movie, so think carefully!

The same rules apply for any credits you wish to include. Often just a few still credits at the end look effective, but classic rolling credits work just as well if you have a lot to get through.

EXPORTING YOUR FINAL FILM

Once you're happy with all of the elements of your final film, you are ready to 'export' it. Exporting is the term we use for turning your editing project into a digital file that can be shared, posted online, burnt to disk or simply viewed on a computer. Most apps support a variety of file types and will have a very clear process for you to follow. Typically, you'll find a button or menu that says 'share',

'export', 'finalise' or something similar. Again, specific instructions for your device or application can be found online.

At the end of this process you will have a file on your device or computer that contains the completed version of your film, ready for you to share with the world.

SHOW OFF YOUR FILM

Congratulations, your film is finished! You should be proud of what you've created. You've experimented with new ideas and skills to create your first movie. The next thing to do is to show all of your friends, family and anyone else out there who might like to see your film.

GETTING YOUR WORK ONLINE

The easiest way to show off your work is by putting it up online for people to see. There are many sites to do this, but the biggest are YouTube and Vimeo. YouTube is the biggest online video website in the world, with millions of videos.

Vimeo is another video website that you might have heard of. Unlike YouTube, it has been designed for professionals to upload their work. Vimeo has a great online filmmaking community that can offer really useful tips to improve your work in the future.

Both sites are very easy to use. It's as simple as finding the video file you exported on the computer and selecting it from inside the upload page on either YouTube or Vimeo.

THIS PROCESS IS SIMILAR TO UPLOADING A PICTURE ON FACEBOOK OR TWITTER ALTHOUGH IT DOES TAKE A LITTLE BIT LONGER AS THE FILES ARE MUCH BIGGER.

ADVANCED UPLOADING

When you upload a video, the website will convert it into the format that it prefers before making it visible online. This can mean losing some quality in the final version, but you can minimise this by changing the way you upload. It's a little more complicated, and the exact steps to follow depend on what editing software you use.

If done correctly, your uploaded video should be almost exactly the same quality as what you saw when editing.

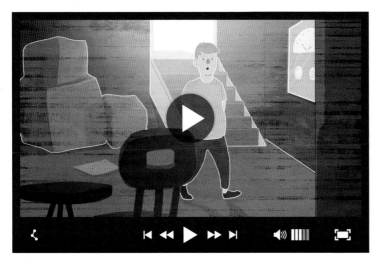

Whilst the degraded, low-quality look might have its appeal for certain types of projects, it's always best to add it in as an effect on your editing program, rather than leaving it to mistakes in the uploading process.

HANDY TIP!
If you are struggling to find the settings you need on your editing software, search the internet for an online video tutorial. You should be able to find a system that works for you.

HOW IT WORKS

Video sites like YouTube and Vimeo use a form of video encoding called 'H.264'. This video setting is capable of creating high-quality videos in really small file sizes, which is why it has become the most used video codec in the world. If you upload a video that is not in this format to YouTube or Vimeo, they will convert it automatically.

Luckily, many video editing programs now include presets for these settings. You can also use full manual control to allow you to upload to websites without them re-converting your video.

HANDY TIP!
If you're using another program but cannot find direct YouTube or Vimeo options then a good rule of thumb is to look for settings with these keywords: web, H.264 or .mp4.

USING SOCIAL MEDIA

Once you've got the file format sorted, you can share your film in any way you like. This means posting it online on independent filming blogs and forums, emailing it to friends and family, and of course getting it out over social media.

A social network can be a good place to share your work. It will be one of the most successful ways to get your work seen by many people, as your friends and family will be interested to see what you have achieved. You will

likely get some good feedback from it too! There is no doubt that having your work on whatever social networking sites you use can be a great way to get your name out there.

Another upside to this is that you might discover friends with a secret desire to act or work in films. Having your friends – and their friends too – see your work could lead to more casting and crew choices for your next project. The more people who know you make films, the better.

HANDY TIP!
If people around you know that you make films, it might lead to a paid project that can help you to buy new equipment or to make a bigger film for your next project.

STAY SAFE ON THE INTERNET - DON'T GIVE OUT YOUR CONTACT DETAILS TO PEOPLE YOU DON'T KNOW.

ONLINE COMMUNITIES

Feedback from friends and family is great, but it won't be as useful to you as the feedback you might get from filmmaking forums such as Vimeo. The people who will view your work on those sites are also filmmakers and have a little more insight into the subject. They also don't know you personally, so won't be shy about offering constructive criticism!

COMPETITIONS

Why not try entering your film in a competition? You may not be ready for the Oscars, but there are many different competitions out there, and some are aimed specifically at young filmmakers. Even if you don't win, entering one of these competitions can be a great way to get more people to see your film. You may even pick up some useful tips from the winners!

LOCAL FILM FESTIVALS

Another way to get your film out there is by entering it for film festivals. Major cities tend to have hundreds of minor and major film festivals that you can enter your work into, but even in more rural areas there are usually one or two that might be worth entering.

Remember that film festivals are often set up by established filmmakers within your local community. The level of work is usually quite high, but this is nothing to be worried about; most filmmakers want to see the work of others and give helpful tips where possible.

LOCAL FILM FESTIVAL
WORLD PREMIER
YOUR SHORT FILM
TONIGHT ONLY

FILM FESTIVALS ARE A GREAT PLACE TO MEET OTHER LIKE-MINDED PEOPLE AND SWAP STRATEGIES. YOU MIGHT MAKE NEW FRIENDS THAT YOU CAN WORK WITH IN THE FUTURE, OR TAKE INSPIRATION FROM VIEWING OTHER PEOPLE'S WORK.

KEEP ON FILMING!

You are now a filmmaker, and you have worked hard to be able to call yourself that, so you should feel very proud. Take a moment to savour that, and then start thinking about the future. Where you go from here is completely down to you. Could you experiment with other types of film? Begin a new project? Extend the project you have already created? It's your choice.

Before you move on, though, it might be useful to take a look back at your first project and make some notes. What went well, and what didn't? What lessons can you take from your experience that might be useful when making your next film? Is there anything you weren't able to accomplish that you'd like to try again?

- -

48-HOUR FILM CHALLENGE

If you're struggling to come up with a new direction, my suggestion would be to set yourself challenges. My favourite thing to do within filmmaking is to work on what is called a 48-hour Film Challenge.

HOW IT WORKS

Some organisations run official 48-hour challenges, but you can do it on your own. All you have to do is make a short film of 2-5 minutes in length that follows some pre-decided guidelines. Students are given a set of narrative prompts at the start of the challenge and then exactly 48 hours later they have to hand in their film.

I DO THESE CHALLENGES WITH MY STUDENTS AS THEY ARE FAST, FUN, REWARDING, AND GIVE YOU A REAL SENSE OF ACCOMPLISHMENT.

A 48-hour film challenge might seem daunting, but it forces you to think quickly and go with your gut instincts. It's great fun to do with a small group of friends and can be a really exciting way to make a short film.

One thing you can do to make your job easier is to find cast and locations before starting the challenge. This will save time but also help you in coming up with your story as your actors, locations and mystery narrative prompts will guide your ideas towards a certain type of film.

Film Challenge!
Title: The Last Lemon
Prop: large suitcase
Line: 'Is that the best you've got?'
Shot: dolly zoom

Use these elements in your film.
You have 48 hours!

HANDY TIP!
Use the lessons you learned in your first film to set yourself specific challenges for your next production.

Movie making skills you can apply to the challenge

Re-use your contacts – If an actor, location or crew member worked well last time, use them again for your challenge.

Script writing – Quickly put together a workable script in a professional format to make it easily understood by your cast and crew.

Planning – Use your experience in planning to get the important elements put together quickly. Plan filming times, and make a rough list of shots, props and costumes. Make sure you have a plan for where you will come up with your idea, where you will be filming and, finally, where you will be editing.

Handheld techniques – Use your skills to move from shot to shot faster by shooting with controlled handheld. It might not be as clean as a tripod, but you can get more shots completed in the time period.

Streamline your editing process – If possible, begin working on editing or uploading your footage to your device as soon as possible. Laptop and tablet users could get the edge on this type of challenge by editing on the bus ride home.

HANDY TIP!
To get your own 48-hour brief, you can ask someone to come up with the narrative props that you will use, or use an online generator website to give you a randomised title, line of dialogue, and specific shot. These are easy to find online.

BUILDING YOUR PORTFOLIO

If you have really enjoyed making your film, it might be something that becomes a lifelong passion. If you want a career in this area, your passion will motivate you to work on more and more projects and improve your portfolio.

I would suggest making one film for yourself, and then another film for someone else. You will likely have friends that are in a band, or starting one up. If you approach your friends and offer to make music videos for them, it not only gives you more experience, but it could also lead to your first paid job.

EXPERIMENT AS MUCH AS POSSIBLE AND TRY OUT NEW TECHNIQUES AS YOU CONTINUE MAKING MOVIES.

FINDING OUT MORE

As a final word, there is a wealth of information out there about learning to make films. This book has been designed to help those starting with zero experience and to guide you through the process of your first film. This is really only the beginning and I recommend that you keep experimenting and trying out new techniques as you continue making movies. You have what you need to get started. I wish you the best of luck!

GLOSSARY

3-POINT LIGHTING A basic lighting technique using 3 lights to separate the foreground, midground and background from each other.

180 DEGREE RULE A filming technique designed to keep characters on their own side of the screen throughout a scene to minimise confusion.

BUDGET A breakdown of the foreseeable costs within a project.

CONTRAST The difference between the brightest and darkest parts of an image. High contrast images have both very bright and very dark areas.

CREW The production team responsible for the practical jobs needed to film a scene.

CUTAWAY Footage used to look away from the main story of a scene, to cover up edit points.

DEPTH How distance is highlighted within a scene. Lighting, the layering of props and camera focus can help to illustrate depth within an image.

DOCUMENTARY A factual film.

DOLLY A piece of film equipment consisting of a moving platform mounted onto a track, from which scenes can be shot to give the camera a smooth motion.

FOUND-FOOTAGE Old or amateur film that is used in another film, or a movie that is made to look like it's been filmed by the characters in the story.

HANDHELD A camera technique using the hands, arms and body to support the weight of the camera and control its motion.

HD Stands for 'High Definition'. HD is used to describe video of a higher resolution than standard definition.

KEY DIAGRAM A basic illustration of how the characters and camera move around the scene – usually a bird's eye view of the set or location.

LENS The imaging elements of a camera usually made from glass that receive and focus light from the surrounding environment in order to produce an image. Lenses often have control of their internal elements on their exterior for use by the camera operator.

LOCATION The area in which a scene or film will be shot. Locations are noted as interior (INT) or exterior (EXT) on production paperwork depending on whether they are inside or outside.

MASTER SHOT The name given to a shot that incorporates all of the action within a scene from start to finish, from the widest perspective planned.

NON-LINEAR EDITING A video-editing technique that allows the user to make infinite changes without destroying or 'cutting' the original image.

PORTFOLIO The professional collection of work completed by a filmmaker, used to display their talents and abilities to others in order to help them find new filmmaking jobs.

PRODUCTION VALUE How professional a film looks. High production value films look like they cost more money to make than they actually did.

REFLECTOR A piece of filmmaking equipment that acts a bit like a large mirror and is used to reflect and direct light into a scene. It can be used with natural and artificial light.

RIGGING A broad term given to filming equipment used to suspend the camera for a specific practical use. Examples of rigging include cranes zip wires, and camera stabilisers.

SHOOTING SCRIPT A list of shots planned for a filming session.

SHOT One planned take within your film.

STABILISER A form of camera rigging designed to help control handheld shots to give a smoother handheld motion.

STOP-MOTION An animation technique used to make it seem like an object is moving on its own. The object is moved a tiny amount between each shot, and then all the shots are joined together to make a film.

STORYBOARD Similar to a cartoon strip, a storyboard is an illustration of the planned shots in a scene to help the cast and crew members visualise how the scene should be filmed.

TONE A term used to describe the emotional undercurrent of a film through its script, performances, editing, colour or music.

TRAILER A collection of shots and sequences advertising the full film, to grab the interest of potential audiences.

ZOOM The camera function used for moving from wider to closer framed shots, within the same continuous take.

INDEX